Opening up Judaism

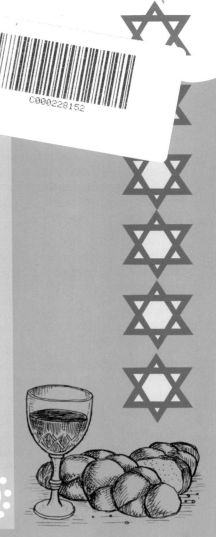

At the heart of Judaism are the ideas of tradition, family and identity. Th[e] challenge for teachers when teaching about Judaism is to pass on the [spirit] of the Jewish community. The spirit of the religion can be lost if teachin[g] is focused on the rules and regulations of Judaism or if the learning is to[o] carefully demarcated into festival, story or belief.

In this book we have tried to share the voices of some members of the Jewish community. Isabel talks about Rosh Hashanah, Jewish children share their thoughts about the synagogue, and Holocaust survivors explain why they remain faithful to Judaism.

We also look at some key themes within Judaism. The importance of a special day of refreshment and rest each week is explored through dance, discussion and art. The importance of the synagogue as a 'home from home' central to the worshipping community, but for much more than worship, is shared through an exploration of Northwood and Pinner Liberal Synagogue.

When teaching 9–11 year olds we are aware that many teachers cover Judaism when they are teaching about the Second World War. We were concerned to ensure that Jewish people are represented as members of living, vibrant, thriving communities and not only as victims. 'Why continue being Jewish?' is a unit of work that grapples with big RE questions while exploring the challenges of belonging to a religious community.

For the subject leader we have provided a set of pages to improve teachers' understanding of Judaism and to support them in teaching about and from Judaism accurately and appropriately. The support and guidance of Lisa Kassapian, our faith community consultant, has been invaluable, ensuring we have represented Judaism in Britain today.

Fiona Moss
Editor

Web links: RE Today website

The RE Today website offers subscribers some free additional resources and classroom-ready materials related to this publication. Look out for the 'RE Today on the web' logo at the end of selected articles.

To access resources:

- go to the RE Today website www.retoday.org.uk

- click on the **download login** button and use the password from this term's issue of *REtoday* magazine

- click on **Primary curriculum publication – web supplement**

- click on the title of the publication and scroll down the page to find what you are looking for.

Contents

SHABBAT: A SPECIAL TIME

For the teacher

Shabbat, or the Sabbath, is a special time for Jewish people. It is the highlight of the week, to be eagerly anticipated through the week and treasured afterwards.

This day of rest and refreshment gives a rhythm to the lives of many Jews. It brings them back to their families and reminds them of their place within a wider religious tradition.

For young children, this unit focuses on three ideas and explores how they are celebrated in Shabbat and also makes links with children's own experience.

Welcoming: Preparing for Shabbat is like getting ready for a special guest. Children can explore what this is like.

Resting: Shabbat gives a space for people to break off from busy lives and recharge their batteries. It is seen as a day of delight. Children can explore how delightful it is to rest.

Treasuring: The joy of Shabbat is something that is not only remembered through the week – Jewish people treasure the memory and the experience. Children can think about how some things are worth treasuring.

The work in this unit is based on work from Angela Daniels, Kingsland CE Primary School, Herefordshire

Information file

Shabbat plays a central part in Jewish practice, with a particular relevance for the role of the family. It links with the story of the Jews escaping from slavery in Egypt. God provided them with bread (manna) and on the sixth day he gave them double the amount so that they wouldn't have to work on the Sabbath.

It also relates to the seventh day of creation, where God rested from his work. This is not seen in a negative sense of being prevented from doing what Jewish people would really like to do, but in a very positive sense of resting from the busy-ness of life and enjoying rest and fun with their families.

There are some key rituals that take place, including the lighting of candles, the eating of bread, sharing wine, reciting blessings and singing together. The role of the mother is particularly important in Shabbat celebrations.

What can children do as a result of this unit?

These pupil-friendly 'I can . . .' statements describe what pupils working at levels 1 and 2 may achieve through this work.

Level   Description of achievement: I can. . .

1
- say something about what Jewish people do to get ready for Shabbat
- ask a question about how Jewish people treasure the special time of Shabbat
- *talk about how good it is to have rest and fun, for Jewish people and for me*
- *talk about how I welcome people.*

2
- think of some questions to ask a Jewish person
- say what makes Shabbat special to Jewish people
- *give two answers to the questions, 'Why is a day of rest a special gift for Jewish people? Is it a special gift for me?'*

RE Today Services

Activity 1
Introduction: a special bubble

Blow some bubbles and invite the children to imagine that they are inside one of these bubbles.

Talk about:

- What does it feel like?

- Would you like anyone else in there with you? Who?

- What would you be glad to get away from if you were floating away in one of these bubbles?

- Would you need to take anything into the bubble with you? Be careful: if you take too much it may burst!

The children may like to draw a picture or write a poem based on these thoughts.

Discuss whether the children have ever felt separated from the normal, ordinary things that they do, times when they have been content, happy, floating. Share some special moments. What made them special?

Activity 2   Welcoming Part 1
Preparing for Shabbat: welcoming the Day of Delight

Explain that Jewish people have a very special 'bubble' time each week. They call it Shabbat, a **holy** time, when they can think about God and their family. On this day some Jews don't do any work at all so that they can really rest. For religious people, 'holy' means very special, separate and different.

Talk about:

- What work would need to be done before if you were all going to have a rest – Mum and Dad too!?

Ask the pupils:

- Do you sometimes have to do extra work so that you can really enjoy a special day? e.g. packing to go on holiday, doing your homework as soon as you get in so that you can go to a party.

It is a bit like getting ready for the Queen to come. What would you do if the Queen was coming to the classroom, or to your house? e.g. spend time tidying, cleaning, making sure you look smart, putting away your things, shopping for lovely food, preparing it, laying a table.

Arrange for a special visitor to come to the class.

Ask the children to tidy up the classroom, ready for the special visitor, and talk about why they are doing this. Why do people make special preparations for a visitor?

Activity 3   Welcoming Part 2   Roleplay Shabbat meal

Jewish people lay the table in a special way with candles and bread. Watch a clip to show what happens in many Jewish homes (for example, BBC Learning Zone clips 3874, 3875 or 4745.)

Role-play the ceremony at the beginning of Shabbat, at sunset on Friday evening.

Talk about:

- the two loaves and the story of the Jews escaping from slavery in Egypt. Explain that God provided them with bread (manna) and that on the sixth day he gave them double the amount so that they wouldn't have to work on the Sabbath.

- the Kiddush prayers and cup of wine which the family all share. This is a sign of joy and oneness within the family.

  ◦ Is there a time when you share something with your family and you feel really close and together? e.g. a meal, a walk, a celebration?

- the candles which are lit by the mother as she welcomes the light and warmth to fill the hearts of all the family.

  ◦ What makes you feel warm and bright inside?

- the blessing which is said by the parents to the children:

  May the Lord bless you and keep you
  May the Lord let His face shine upon you and be gracious to you
  May the Lord look kindly upon you and give you peace

  (Numbers 6:24-26)

Work together as a class to write a blessing (good wishes) for a member of the school family.

Activity 4
Busy busy!

Think together with the pupils about:

- Weekly routines: having to get to school on time, the school bell and the order of the school day, home time and times of after-school activities, teatime and bedtime.

- Consider when we are 'free' of these routines e.g. holidays and weekends. Do you like holidays? Why?

Share busy-ness through dance:
Ask the children, in groups, to 'become' a repetitive machine.

- What sort of movements might they choose?

- How do they work together?

Put the dance to some suitable repetitive, 'mechanical' music. For example, John Adams' *Short Ride in a Fast Machine*.

Change the style of music to something much more free and fun, for example, Rimsky Korsakov's *Scheherazade* 3rd Movement.

See: http://tinyurl.com/3or3onq

Ask the children to develop their own movements to this different style of music.

Ask how the children felt in both dance activities.

- Did they feel more free/independent/creative in the second one?

- What would happen if they stayed in the first dance all the time?

If a week can be like the first dance, with all the busy things they have to do, why would it be a good idea to have a rest at the weekend? (To stop the busy things and rest, but also to be free to choose what to do.)

Activity 5
Resting on the Day of Delight

Show the pupils a copy of the Torah and share the story of creation as understood by Jews in Genesis, chapter 1.

Genesis 2:1-3 God rested on the seventh day. In the 4th commandment, Jews are commanded to remember the Sabbath (Exodus 20: 8-10).

- Why do you think God commanded that Shabbat should be holy?

Use the bubble sheet on page 6. Remind pupils about the idea of time out from the busy week as a kind of bubble.

Ask the pupils to draw a picture of them doing something which they really enjoy, **apart from** something to do with a 'machine' such as television, computer games, videos or mechanised transport.

Discuss the pictures they draw.

- Are they with anyone else?

- Talking? Reading? Playing? Walking? Eating? Thinking?

- What makes these times special? Draw up a list.

Explain that Jewish people will spend Shabbat in a special way: it is a day of rest, fun and prayer. Some Jewish people will go to the synagogue, some may think about God and some will enjoy being with their families. Many Jewish people will find a way of helping others. It is a day of joy and peace. Jewish people throughout the world are like a big family, especially when they share Shabbat.

Ask the pupils to draw some of the things that Jewish people do in their 'bubble' of Shabbat.

BBC Learning Zone clips library clip 3877 shows two young girls going to synagogue on Shabbat.

- Watch the clip and then see how many of the things that children identified in their pictures above were shown in the clip.

- Why do these girls enjoy going to synagogue?

4

Activity 6
Treasuring the Day of Delight

If possible start this activity after a break or lunchtime, creating the smell of spices in the classroom for when children return. An incense stick would work, ideally with a smell of cinnamon or cloves. This will link with the activity below.

Blow a few more bubbles and let them burst. That's the trouble with bubbles – they don't last very long!

Remember the idea that Shabbat is like a bubble of rest and joy in the midst of a busy week. Jewish people do several things to make the bubble linger into the day ahead.

Watch a short video clip (e.g. number 3968 on the BBC Learning Zone clips library) to show the Havdalah ceremony.

Note with the pupils

- The smell of spices
- Lighting the candle
- The overflowing cup

Talk about

- How might these help Jewish people to carry the Shabbat into the week?
- What is the difference between treasuring and remembering?
- What do you treasure? How do you show this?

Jewish people treasure the special time of Shabbat.

Talk about

- How do you treasure special times?
- Do you have photographs or souvenirs?
- Can you remember the smell of certain places?
- Is there some music that reminds you of a special time?

Talk about the spices that filled the room when the children entered.

- How might that be a good way of remembering and treasuring a special time?

Activity 7   Treasuring

The spice boxes used at Shabbat are often beautifully decorated. Pupils could look at some pictures of some spice boxes.

An internet search will show a range of these, or look at the very exotic collection at www.judaism.com under Judaica > Shabbat & Holidays > Havdalah sets.

See: http://tinyurl.com/3mb2fmn

Copy the net on page 7 onto card.

Ask pupils to make a simple 'spice box' of their own.

- Cut out the net
- Decorate the box on the shaded parts
- Stick the box together
- Cut out the crown and stick it on the top of the spice box.

Inside their box, children can put a picture or word to represent something they treasure.

Alternatively, for very young children, ask them to bring in a small box to decorate with coloured tissue paper, etc.

Remember that some Jewish people welcome the Sabbath Queen, as if greeting a special guest.

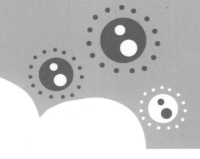

Shabbat bubble

Bubble 1 My special time

Bubble 2 Shabbat

RE Today
Services

Spice box net

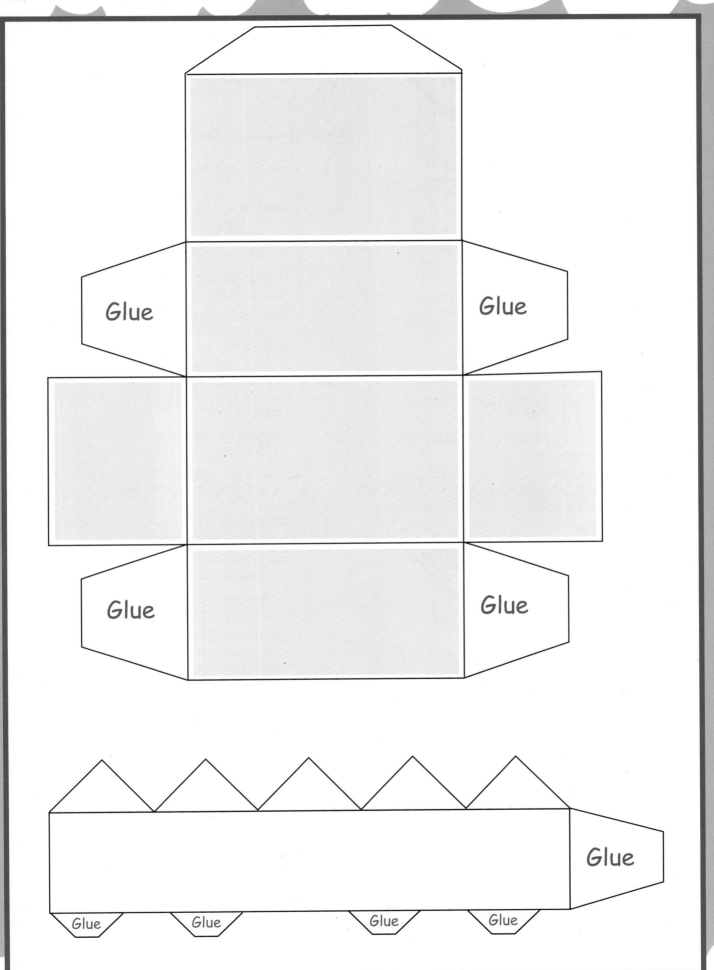

THE SYNAGOGUE: JOINING IN

For the teacher

Learning about and learning from the range of buildings known as 'synagogues' can provide pupils with an introduction to some of the common elements in the practices and way of life of this diverse religion. The synagogue brings the Jewish community together to pray to God, to learn and share ideas, to meet friends and family and to celebrate special occasions.

The three activities in this section explore how the synagogue is central to the worshipping Jewish community, a home from home. The activities enable pupils to:

- find out about a visit to a synagogue
- listen to what some Jewish children say about the synagogue
- learn about how some Jewish people welcome a new baby
- reflect on a Jewish story to consider personal spaces and sacred places
- consider what is special and what makes them thankful about their home.

Information file

The synagogue is commonly known by the Yiddish word 'shul', from the German for 'school'. It is also referred to by three Hebrew names:

- *beit tefillah* – House of Prayer
- *beit k'nesset* – House of Assembly
- *beit midrash'* – House of Learning.

There are two main movements within Judaism: **orthodox** (which includes Hasidic) and **progressive** (which includes liberal and reform). Most Jews living in the UK belong to one of these two movements.

Both branches believe in the importance of the Torah, but they place different emphases on it. This is seen in some everyday synagogue practice, for example:

- in **orthodox synagogues** men and women sit separately for prayers, only men may lead worship and only men can become rabbis.
- in **progressive synagogues** men and women sit together, both may lead worship and women may become rabbis.

Achievements and outcomes

These pupil friendly 'I can . . .' statements suggest the learning outcomes that this work can yield.

Level	Description of achievement: I can. . .
1	• **recall** a traditional Jewish folktale about a rabbi • **use the right words to** name some features of synagogues and some things which are special to Jewish people, such as the ark, mezuzah, tallit • **recognise symbols** of Judaism seen in the synagogue • *talk* about their own experiences of being in noisy and crowded places and of having space to think.
2	• **use religious words** to identify some symbols used in the Jewish religion and some special religious clothing • **suggest meanings** for religious symbols such as the *ner tamid* – everlasting light • *express* empathy with the experiences of others as they listen to the story
3	• **identify** a variety of ways in which Jewish people may be part of the synagogue • **describe** some ways in which respect for God is expressed in the synagogue • **make links** between the use of the tallith and the idea of personal space • *identify* ways in which they should be thankful and say who and what influences their attitudes and behaviour.

The following resources are available for subscribers to download from the RE Today website.

- pictures and descriptions for Activity 2
- picture of the synagogue doors
- a longer version of the story 'The House with no Room'

See: www.retoday.org.uk

Activity 1   The synagogue – a house of prayer

This activity invites pupils to find out about the synagogue as a 'house of prayer' by looking at the symbolism seen by visitors and experienced by members of the Jewish community.

- **Prepare** the class for a visit to a synagogue or to meet a member of the Jewish faith. Put together questions that they want to ask. Encourage the pupils to ask questions themselves.

- **Visit** a synagogue and discuss the symbols and or any symbolic actions observed (page 10).

- **Select** the words which they think will apply to the synagogue before their visit. Choose the most appropriate adjectives after the visit. Compare the expectations and the experience (page 10).

- **Discuss** the symbolism behind what is seen either first-hand or through a virtual tour, using artefacts, posters and pictures and building on pupils' experiences.

- **Paint/draw** a picture of a scene from the synagogue in which signs and symbols are seen. Write about the picture using some correct religious words.

- **Draw**, or reproduce using modelling materials, one of the artefacts described by Jewish children (page 10), describe the symbols and create own symbols to illustrate a Jewish belief or action.

Outside the synagogue

- Have a look at some of the writing on the outside of the building.

- See if you can find out what the writing means.

- What can you see on the door frame of the synagogue? Where else might this be seen?

Through the doors of the synagogue

- Can you find . . . a Jewish symbol, e.g. a Star of David or menorah?

- What is above the doors of the ark? Some writing? Images? The ner tamid (everlasting light)?

- Can you find the Torah scroll? Is there more than one Torah? Is there a yad (pointer)?

- Can you find any other books? What are they? Where are they?

- Choose a window and describe what you can see, e.g. colours, patterns, writing.

- Look at the noticeboard. What activities might happen in the synagogue other than worship?

Meeting a member of the Jewish community

- Who is the person in charge of their synagogue? What rules do they follow? Why do they want to belong to the worshipping community?

- What signs show that they belong (e.g. Star of David, kippah, tzitzit, tallit)

- How does their faith affect the way they behave?

> The synagogue is very important for me because it allows me to mix with other Jewish people.
> It is a place I feel very comfortable in – a home from home! All the people in my synagogue make it such an amazing place to be.

The following words were used by young synagogue members to describe the atmosphere inside their place of worship.

Ask children to choose five words that they think will describe the synagogue
- before the visit or virtual visit
- after the visit or virtual visit

Children and teachers can also add their own words to the list, before and after their visit.

musical	colourful	silent	loud	quiet
friendly	special	peaceful	happy	sad
serious	enjoyable	exciting	cool	welcoming
caring	joyful	warm	safe	loving

RE Today
Services

Activity 2 Through the doors of Northwood and Pinner Liberal Synagogue

Share the descriptions of key features of the synagogue given by some Jewish children below.

Ask the children to

- **talk about** the descriptions of key features given below
- work in pairs to match the photographs with the description of some key features of a synagogue
- choose a key feature to sketch and label
- **discuss** why the item is symbolic or important.

'There is a box where men and boys can take a **kippah**, a small hat used to cover their heads when they pray.'	**Some Jewish children explain about key features of the synagogue**	'The **Torah** scrolls are decorated with pictures like the tree of life and shining silver crowns. These make a jangling noise when they are moved. When the Torah is seen we all stand up and we say a prayer together in Hebrew.'
'The **ner tamid** (eternal light) is a light which is always shining above the Ark, it reminds the Jewish people that God is always with them. The everlasting light shows that God is everlasting love and light.'	'The Ark is like a secret cupboard. Our Ark is quite plain. When the doors are opened there is a light inside and golden silk curtains spread warmness. The Ark feels cared for. When the curtains open I can see the Torah scrolls.'	'When the Torah is read, it must not be touched. We use a special pointer with a tiny silver hand at the top. It is called a **yad**.'
	**Photos to match, sketch and label**	

Photos © Lisa Kassapian

© 2011 RE Today Services
Permission is granted to photocopy this page for use in classroom activities in schools that have purchased this publication.

RE Today Services

Activity 3 Welcoming in – opening the door

Above the doors of this synagogue are some Hebrew words. They tell visitors that this is a very special place for all Jewish people, no matter where in the world they come from.

Ask pupils to

- **reflect** on the place where they live.

- **discuss** what message they would write for visitors above the door of their home?

- **design a banner** showing a welcome message to the classroom.

Show the pupils the right-hand side of the doorpost of the synagogue. Can they see a small box? It is a mezuzah. Inside is a tiny scroll with a prayer from the Torah called the Shema.

Explain that the words inside the mezuzah tell Jewish people:

'You shall love the Lord with all your heart, with all your soul and with everything you have.'

The words are so important that the Shema tells Jewish people to:

'Teach them carefully to your children. Speak of them when you are sitting at home and when you are travelling, when you go to bed and when you get up . . . Write them on the doorposts of your house and on your gate posts.'

Ask pupils to

- **think about** important words and promises that they have made, heard or know that other people make.

- **make** individual promise containers using, for example, empty glue stick holders. Alternatively create a whole class promise box.

- **examine the** symbolic behaviour of a practising Jewish person passing the mezuzah on their house or synagogue door, e.g. on the *Jewish Way of Life* CD-ROM.

These quotes show what some Jewish people like about their synagogue.
Share these with your children.
- What did they like about the synagogue?
- What surprised them?
- What did they learn?

. . . the Rabbi makes it fun for different people. He helps you to understand the language because we pray in Hebrew. I go to Cheder on Sunday mornings to learn to read and write Hebrew, some grown ups still go to synagogue to learn Hebrew.

. . . listening to music, looking at the banners and praying.

. . . dressing up when we celebrate Purim.

. . . when we light the candles, it says that the world is light and it makes you feel warm inside.

Activity 4 Welcoming a baby

Babies born in the Jewish faith are welcomed in different ways into their community. Baby Rosie has been blessed by the Rabbi (teacher) with her brother and sister as part of the Sabbath morning service in the synagogue. The Rabbi asks their parents to make sure that the children will learn about the Jewish faith at home and in the synagogue. Jewish children come to the synagogue to pray, to meet people, to celebrate and to learn. The members of the synagogue welcome the new baby. After the service they share food and drinks together.

Ask the pupils

- How are new babies welcomed in other religions? Have you ever been to any baby-welcoming ceremonies?

- Why do Jewish people want to bless a new baby?

- What sort of blessings might a Jewish person want for a child?

I liked going up (on the Bimah), there were lots and lots of people looking at us. The Rabbi asked me some questions. I saw the choir singing, I like being able to sing. There was a cupboard (the Ark), inside was the scroll (the Torah). The Rabbi took it out and read it. You have to touch it very gently. The Rabbi read in Hebrew . . .
I know some Hebrew, like the blessings for the wine and the bread . . . When they read in synagogue they say my name a lot, because it is one of the fathers for the Jewish people. It makes me feel special.
Jacob, age 7

The baby blessing was exciting and everyone sang. I was quite nervous. I like it in the synagogue. There is a lot of music, it is a happy place but quiet sometimes too. When it is too loud I can't think. It is quiet when we pray to God at the synagogue. I say thank you to God because he made people, like my little sister.
Hannah, age 6

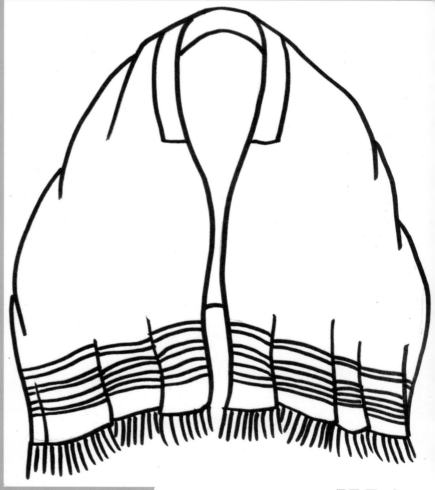

RE Today
Services

Activity 5   A house with no room

A synagogue is a 'house of learning' and in this activity pupils share a story based on a Jewish folk tale from Eastern Europe. Pupils think about being grateful for what they have. They focus on the tallit as a sacred space.

The story is retold in two picture books

- *The Little House* by Erica Gordon and Victor Ambrus, ISBN 978-0-216-93015-5
- *It Could Always Be Worse: A Yiddish Folk Tale*, by Margot Zemach, ISBN 978-0-374-43636-0

Ask children to

- **think about** their homes, consider times when things are noisy or quiet, when the house feels crowded or empty. Do they have a special space where they can be quiet and think?

- **listen** to the story and talk together about the Rabbi's advice, what surprised them and why did the Rabbi make this suggestion, what did the farmers learn from their actions?

- **experience** what it feels like to be alone in a small space. Use a pop-up tent or create a small den using chairs and a sheet, allow one child to be joined by 3 or 4 others who then leave one by one. Talk about what it feels like to be crowded and then alone.

- **explore** an artefact – the tallit or prayer shawl worn by Jewish men when praying. Explain that *tal* means tent and *lith* means little. The shawl can provide a little tent to create a special place to pray, to think and be alone with God. Create a 'thoughtful area' where children can try on a shawl and sit quietly to reflect.

- **write** inside the prayer shawl template (page 12) what they think that they should be thankful for.

The House with No Room

On a far-away mountain in a far-away village of a far-away country lived a wise, wise, man by the name of Jacob. This wise, wise man was a rabbi. One Sabbath, after synagogue, the village farmer stopped him.

'Wise Rabbi,' he said, 'do help me, please, my house is so small, there's no room to breathe.'

So the wise Rabbi followed the farmer to his house and they squeezed into the tiny kitchen where his wife and children were eating lunch. Rabbi Jacob tugged at his beard thoughtfully.

'Yes!' he exclaimed, 'Your house is small – it is plain to see, so you must invite all your animals for tea! Give them your beds to stay for the night. God bless you all, I hope you sleep tight.'

In disbelief, the farmer and his wife followed the Rabbi's advice and brought all of their animals into the house. The tiny house was crammed to the rafters. Nobody slept, nobody ate.

The Rabbi was asked for advice once again, 'Take them out one by one and put an end to your pain.'

'Get them out,' cried the farmer, 'before it's too late!' Together they pushed out at first just one cow. The house seemed a tiny bit bigger by now. The poor family still could not sleep with their bedroom full of goats and sheep! Gradually, day by day, all of the animals were taken away.

Finally, as the last animal was led back to the farmyard, the farmer and his family stood and admired the emptiness. All of a sudden the house wasn't small any longer: there was space in the beds and space on the floor. The farmer, his wife and their children danced through their lovely house enjoying the room to breathe.

The following Sabbath at synagogue the family thanked the wise, wise Rabbi for helping them to see what was already theirs and they thanked God for everything they had.

Lisa Kassapian, based on a Jewish folk tale from Eastern Europe

A longer version of this story is available for subscribers
See: www.retoday.org.uk

RE Today
Services

Rosh Hashanah and Yom Kippur: Forgiveness and New Beginnings

For the teacher

Rosh Hashanah and Yom Kippur are the most important festivals in the Jewish year, with their focus on the themes of forgiveness, repentance and reconciliation.

The story of Jonah is told in this unit. A creative way of engaging with this story is outlined to help pupils understand the importance of the story for Jewish people. This is an extremely significant story for Jewish people at this festival time and it is read in full at Yom Kippur.

The activities in this unit focus on the meaning of the festivals of Rosh Hashanah and Yom Kippur to Jewish people today. Pupils are encouraged to consider the relevance of the themes of the festivals to themselves with opportunities for solemn reflection.

Information file: Rosh Hashanah

Rosh Hashanah is a two-day festival that celebrates the creation of the world. It is celebrated in September or October.

Rosh Hashanah is described in Jewish liturgy as 'the day of judgement'. It is a time to consider the good and bad things that have been done over the previous year. Jews believe that God balances a person's good deeds over the last year against their bad deeds, and decides what the next year will be like for them. Jewish people also use this as a time to re-prioritise things in their life.

Time is spent in the synagogue at Rosh Hashanah where prayers of thanks are said for the good things of the previous year. Other prayers ask for a good and peaceful year. The shofar, ram's horn, is also blown; 100 notes are played in a special rhythm to announce the new year, to remind Jews that God is their ruler and judge and to warn them that they need to improve.

At home a meal is shared and prayers are said.

Challah is eaten; it is baked in a circle to remind Jews of the cycle of the year and the cycle of life.

Sweet foods are eaten such as honey cakes, apples dipped in honey, and for some, carrot stew. These reflect the hope of Jewish people that the next year will be good and sweet for them and their loved ones.

Pomegranates are often placed on the meal table; the seeds remind Jewish people of the 613 commandments in the Torah. They are also a reminder of the many good deeds that can be done.

What children can do as a result of this unit

These pupil friendly 'I can . . .' statements suggest the learning outcomes that may be expected of pupils.

Level   Description of achievement: I can. . .

2
- ask questions about the festivals of Rosh Hashanah and Yom Kippur
- talk about the idea of regret and repentance within the festivals
- *respond sensitively to these Jewish festivals sharing what is meaningful to me and actions that I regret.*

3
- ask questions and find answers to questions about the meaning and significance of Rosh Hashanah and Yom Kippur
- make a link between the story of Jonah and the themes of Yom Kippur
- *make a link between what Jewish people do at Rosh Hashanah and Yom Kippur and times when I choose to think about what is meaningful to me and actions that I regret.*

See also

1 BBC Learning Zone Broadband Class Clips
- Rosh Hashanah and Yom Kippur clip 3663
- Jonah clip 3665

See: www.bbc.co.uk/learningzone/clips

2 *Exploring Celebrations*, ed. Joyce Mackley

This publication from RE Today explores how and why religious festivals are important, with practical classroom activities covering five religions.

See : www.retoday.org.uk

3 *Jewish Way of Life* CD

This interactive guide to learning about Judaism and Jewish people is available to schools for free. The section on Festival looks at Rosh Hashanah and Yom Kippur.

See: www.jwol.org.uk

The following resources are available for subscribers to download from the RE Today website.

- PowerPoint presentation introducing the activities
- A4 copy of the food outlines to create the mobile in Activity 1
- large outline of a goat to use in Activity 4

See: www.retoday.org.uk

RE Today Services

What means most to Isabel?

Why are Rosh Hashanah and Yom Kippur such important festivals for Jewish people?

Rosh Hashanah and Yom Kippur are the most important Jewish festivals because they give us a chance to say sorry for the bad things we've done.

We can say sorry to our friends and family for times when we have lost our temper, hurt people or lied. At this time Jewish people have a chance to pray to God so we can say that we are truly sorry and we will make things better if God forgives us.

Rosh Hashanah is a happy celebration because it is the start of a New Year.

After Yom Kippur we feel happy too, because it is like God has given us a second chance and we can have a new beginning.

What special food do you eat at this time?

On Rosh Hashanah we eat Challah bread, which is sweet and round like a crown. We eat honey cakes, which my brother loves. We have pomegranates because they have loads of seeds like the Torah has loads of laws.
The best thing of all is dipping pieces of apple into honey because the honey is sweet and we wish everyone a sweet new year. It's really yummy and sticky, I wish we could have it all the time.
We usually have a special family meal to celebrate and my Grandma always puts out serviettes with Hebrew writing on them and pictures like apples, honey, pomegranates and the shofar.

At Rosh Hashanah all Jewish people think carefully about the past year, reflecting on these questions. Can you tell us how you would answer these questions?

What is the most meaningful thing in my life?
The most meaningful thing in my life is probably my family, but my friends, my school and my dancing are also the most meaningful things.

Who in my life means most to me?
My family means most to me, and my rabbit called Sprinkles.

How often do I tell them?
I tell them that I love them every day.

What are the most significant things I have achieved . . . over the last year?
In the last year I have achieved well in my ballet and tap exams, I performed in a theatre, where I could show everyone what I had learned. I have also improved lots in my swimming and in Maths.

. . . in my life so far?
The most significant things in my life so far have been winning races, winning a competition and taking my dancing exams. I will always remember these things and the holidays that I have had with my family.

Activity 1 Why do we have festivals?

Ask the pupils to

- suggest why religious people have festivals
- suggest some features that are common to more than one festival that they know about

Share the interview with Isabel with the pupils. **Ask them** the following:

- Why are Rosh Hashanah and Yom Kippur important to Isabel?
- How do you think the things Isabel and her family do at these festivals will help them to live good lives?

Split the class into groups and ask them to research the four foods that are mentioned by Isabel: Challah bread, pomegranates, honey cakes and apples. You may want to provide some of these foods for pupils to taste.

Information on these can be found at http://tinyurl.com/6bw552l

Ask the pupils to make a mobile to show some of the important themes of Rosh Hashanah.

Use the four food shapes below to create the mobile. On the back of each food shape ask pupils to explain the significance of the food in this festival.

- When is it eaten?
- Why is it eaten?
- What does it remind Jews of?
- I think Rosh Hashanah is about . . .

Activity 2
Four questions

Both Rosh Hashanah and Yom Kippur are solemn festivals where Jewish people reflect on the year gone by and the year to come.

Reread Isabel's responses to the four questions that lots of Jewish people reflect on at Rosh Hashanah.

- What is Isabel committed to?
- What makes her life meaningful?

Ask the pupils to answer these four questions for themselves.

The pupils may want to keep their answers to themselves or some of them may want to share their ideas and notice the similarities and differences to the responses given by Isabel.

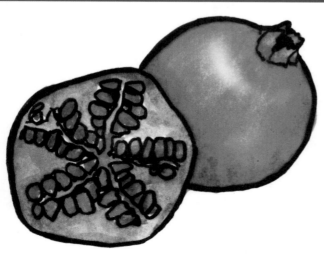

RE Today
Services

Jonah and the Big Fish

One day God spoke to Jonah, 'Go to Nineveh. In this city they are doing many evil and terrible things. Tell them if they do not obey my commandments I will destroy them.' Jonah was petrified and so decided to disobey God and run as far away as possible. He made a journey down to the port and paid his fare for a boat heading to Tarshish. Jonah hoped to be able to escape God completely.

Once he was on the boat he went down into his cabin and fell into a deep sleep. He was exhausted. As he slept, the seas became stormier until eventually the sailors became petrified. The boat was being tossed around and was in serious danger of sinking. Each of the sailors prayed to their own god asking for a solution, the cargo was thrown overboard, but nothing caused the ever-worsening storm to abate.

The captain eventually came into Jonah's cabin and shook him hard until he woke up. The captain begged Jonah to pray to God to find some kind of solution to their terrible situation.

Eventually Jonah blurted out, 'But I can't pray to God because it's him I am trying to run away from.' The sailors soon realised that it was Jonah who was causing the problem, but they weren't sure what to do. They asked Jonah what the solution was, and his reply was 'Throw me over the side.' At first the sailors couldn't bring themselves to throw him over and persevered in trying to row the boat to shore. However, all their efforts were in vain and the storm seemed to get worse.

Eventually they realised that they had to throw Jonah overboard. As they threw him over, they prayed and tried to gain forgiveness from God. As Jonah was pitched overboard God provided a large fish which swam beside the ship and swallowed Jonah. The moment he was thrown overboard the waves subsided and the boat ceased tossing and turning.

Jonah sat inside the big fish, wondering what to do next. If it hadn't been so dark he might have been able to see a way out. As he sat inside the fish he prayed to God, 'Lord thank you for saving me from the swirling seas. Thank you, Lord, for thinking that I am worth saving.' As he lay inside the belly of the fish, hearing strange sounds and fearing the worst, he became more and more scared.

After three days and nights the fish vomited Jonah onto the beach. As he lay on the beach listening to the calm lapping waves and feeling the hot sun, Jonah could not believe how good God had been. His prayers had been heard and answered.

Suddenly Jonah heard God speaking to him again. This time Jonah agreed to go and speak to the people of Nineveh.

Activity 3   Conscience Alley

The book of Jonah is read during the solemn festival of Yom Kippur as a reminder that God is always ready to listen to those who repent of their sins. Read the story of Jonah to the class up to the point where the captain asks Jonah to pray.

Choose a capable speaker and thinker to 'face the dilemma' and play the part of Jonah. Invite four pupils to stand in a line on one side of the alley to explain to Jonah why he should admit his sin to the captain. Invite four pupils to stand on the other side and offer reasons why he should keep quiet. The volunteer Jonah walks the alley, moving from side to side. S/he must ask each pupil, 'What is your advice for me today?' and listen to the replies, asking some 'why' questions and other questions as appropriate. At the end of the alley the teacher must ask Jonah to share what he is going to do and why. What would others do in Jonah's position? Why?

Conclude the activity by reading the rest of the story. What do the pupils think Jewish people can learn from this story?

RE Today
Services

Activity 4 Dealing with our mistakes

Yom Kippur marks the end of the year by dealing with the things that have gone wrong between believers and God. Share with the children something that you have done but regretted.

Ask the pupils to **discuss** with a talk partner:

• Can anything be done about these things?
• What have you done in the past year that you regret?
• What could you do to put it right?

Share with the children information about how Jews mark Yom Kippur, using the 'Information file' and other websites and clips suggested in the resources section at the beginning of this unit.

Ask the pupils to **discuss** with a talk partner:

• Why do Jewish people think it is important to say sorry at least once a year?
• How do you think they feel after this festival?

Draw two large goats on two pieces of paper. Give each child their own goat-shaped piece of paper.

• Think about something the class have done that was not as good as it could have been.
• Write the class regrets on one of the large goats.

Ask the pupils to

• Think about something that they regret doing that they have not put right.
• Write your regret on your own goat silhouette. Explain to the pupils that no one else will read this.
• Stick your regret onto the class goat.

As a class **solemnly** process with the goats and get rid of your regrets in the school bins. This procession should be treated as a time of reflection. The procession or the writing of the regrets could be accompanied by the singing of the Kol Nidrei: an example can be found at http://tinyurl.com/5v9zdsa

Ask pupils to write an acrostic about Rosh Hashanah and Yom Kippur. Use the title SORRY.

'At Rosh Hashanah I go to synagogue. I think about if I have done bad things and what I can do to make myself better for God. We walk to the park, lots of people from our synagogue go there. We take breadcrumbs in a bag and do Tashlich. We throw breadcrumbs into the water – they are like all the bad things that we have done in the past year. We throw all our bad things away and watch them get taken by the water, or eaten by the fish. Me and my family say prayers, we all tell God what we are sorry for, I whisper and think about my new year's resolutions.'

Oliver, 10

Information file: Yom Kippur

At Yom Kippur adults do not eat or drink for a day so they can concentrate on thinking and praying about the things they have done wrong.

In ancient times when the Jewish people lived in the desert, the shofar was blown and two identical goats were brought before the high priest, lots were cast and one goat would be sacrificed to God, the other led to the desert. The high priest placed hands on the goat and said a prayer to say sorry for the things that the people had done wrong. The goat was then sent out into the desert as a symbol that all their collective wrongdoings were disappearing. The goat, which was sacrificed to God, took with it the sins that would be displeasing to God. This was a sign of atonement. When the Jewish people were truly sorry they were able to be 'at one with God'.

Jewish people do not do this now. There are many different ways for them to say sorry to God at Yom Kippur. Some swing money around in a handkerchief over their heads. They say sorry to God and imagine their bad choices being scattered. They will then give the money to charity as a sign of wanting to do better in the future. Others sprinkle breadcrumbs into a river and pray that as the crumbs float away, they will take their bad choices with them.

RE Today Services

THE CREATOR OF THE EARTH? LOOKING AFTER OUR WORLD

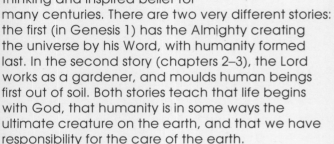

For the teacher

The stories of Genesis chapter 1 and chapters 2 and 3 are often told in RE. These great creation narratives have energised spiritual thinking and inspired belief for many centuries. There are two very different stories: the first (in Genesis 1) has the Almighty creating the universe by his Word, with humanity formed last. In the second story (chapters 2–3), the Lord works as a gardener, and moulds human beings first out of soil. Both stories teach that life begins with God, that humanity is in some ways the ultimate creature on the earth, and that we have responsibility for the care of the earth.

The learning potential of these great stories depends very much on what happens as they are told and responded to. This section of the book provides five activities that enable creative and thoughtful responses to the stories.

It is important to remember that these are Jewish stories first of all. While Christians now share these scriptures with Jewish people, and Muslims list Adam as one of the Prophets of Allah, the Jewish community created, passed on and wrote down these stories. Good RE studies Judaism on its own terms, not through a 'Christian lens', so teachers will want to plan the work on these stories with Jewish understanding in mind. One way of doing this is to respect the Jewish avoidance of writing the holy name of God, using G-d in written form. In Jewish prayers God is addressed through Hebrew words which mean, for example, 'Creator and Sovereign' or 'Eternal One'. In Genesis, God is 'Elohim' (pronounced e lo HEEM), meaning 'the powerful one'. In Judaism, titles are used to emphasise different aspects of God rather than to give God a name.

Creation narratives are controversial, and are used in different ways by creationists, Bible literalists and others. Evolutionary biology tells a different story from Genesis. This is an important area of RE learning, and the final activity in this section will help pupils think about the 'big questions' of origins in the light of scientific understanding. The first activities, though, take the Genesis stories and use them for learning through their narrative power.

This work aims to:

- enable pupils to respond thoughtfully to Jewish stories of the beginning of life on earth

- explore big questions with pupils and allow them to think creatively about: Where do we come from? Why is the world like this? How should we care for our planet? Where did evil come from?

What children can do as a result of this unit

These pupil friendly 'I can . . .' statements suggest the learning outcomes that may be expected of pupils.

Level	Description of achievement: I can. . .
2	• retell a creation story from Jewish holy writings • *respond sensitively to some questions about Jewish stories.*
3	• describe some of the meanings of the stories of creation that Jewish people tell • make connections myself between the stories Jewish people tell, and some ideas about God and about caring for the earth.
4	• show that I understand how Jewish creation stories can make a difference to people caring for the earth • *apply ideas like 'creator', 'big questions' and 'care for the earth' myself, expressing ideas of my own.*

See also

1 **The Torah:** BBC Learning Zone has a five-minute free-to-view programme which makes good connections to the Creation stories in Jewish scripture.

   See: www.bbc.co.uk/learningzone/clips/the torah/7464.html

2 *Picturing Creation* from RE Today. Kate Neal's brilliant artwork inspired by Genesis 1 on disk, video and picture cards, with classroom ideas.

   See: www.retoday.org.uk/shop

3 **Bible Society's 'Empty Hanger' project** asked fashion design students to create costume interpretations of key Bible characters. See what they made of Eve on the RE Today website: www.retoday.org.uk

(W)

Activity 1
Sequence pictures from Genesis 1

Use the 15 clip art images from page 21. One set between three pupils is ideal.

Ask pupils to look at the pictures spread out on the desk, and tell them that all the pictures come in a certain order in the story they are about to hear. Without talking, can they put the 15 pictures in the right order as the story of Genesis 1 is read to them?

Thinking skills activities like this are good for developing an understanding of the story, even though there are no final right answers.

When they have heard the story, groups of three play 'spot the missing two': one pupil takes two of the pictures away, and the others must remember which pictures have gone. If they have the text of the story to look at, this reinforces learning of the story and its sequence.

Activity 2
Suggesting meanings in the story

Use a copy of page 22 for this activity. Cut the page up so that the pupils in groups of three can sequence what goes in each part of the strip.

Give plenty of help with this. Once the first few are done, the rest is easier. The sequencing of Strip 2 is the easiest part of the task. Matching the interpretations in Strip 3 to the questions and 'days' is a bit harder. Answering the questions from Strip 4 is much more difficult.

Using the sheet as a whole, pupils select from Strip 3 their favourite four interpretations. Ask them to suggest some answers to at least three of the questions in Strip 4 – give them a choice about which ones they tackle.

Activity 5
Story-making and creative arts

Ask pupils to write a story of their own, for the twenty-first century.

Title suggestions: 'Temptation', 'Forbidden fruit' or 'One rule'.

Discuss whether these stories will include a divine character – why, or why not?

Using creative arts: Look carefully at some of the great artworks inspired by the Garden of Eden story.

- How do the artists show their ideas and beliefs about God?
- Why is it difficult to picture God?

Create a work of art about the Garden of Eden story yourself: how will you show your beliefs about God through the arts?

Activity 3   Another Jewish creation story: Adam and Eve

The story of Adam and Eve in the Garden of Eden starts at Genesis 2:4b. The story told here, often called 'The Fall', of their taking the forbidden fruit and being punished for their wrongdoing, is found in Genesis 3. A slightly different version of this story can be found in the Qur'an, 20:116 onwards.

Cut page 23 into 12 cards. Tell the story simply.

Ask pupils to

- work in pairs to put the story in the right order
- choose a symbol or image from a clip-art collection to match each part of the story.

Place a chair with a box of fruit on it in a prominent place in the school hall, or where pupils walk out of classes to the playground, with a big notice on it saying: 'It is forbidden to touch this chair'.

Station two pupils with a tick chart nearby, but not obviously involved with the chair, and get them to record how many pupils walking by notice the sign and touch the chair.

It provides a starting point for the idea that 'rules are made to be broken' and that temptation feels strong when something is forbidden – the origin of the idea of 'forbidden fruit' is clearly in Genesis!

The discussion point is that Adam and Eve had one rule, and broke it – but would anyone have done any differently?

Activity 4   Making sense of the story: questions for discussion and writing

1 Why do you think God made the one rule for Eve and Adam?

2 What did Eve do in the story that was wrong? Why was it wrong? How was the serpent involved? How was Adam involved?

3 What was the result of Eve's action? What was the result of Adam's action? What was the result of the serpent's action? What suffering resulted from each of these people's actions?

4 Have you been tempted to do things you knew to be wrong? In what ways have you tempted others to do things you knew to be wrong? Why do we do wrong?

5 When have you successfully resisted temptation to do wrong?

6 What have been the consequences of your wrongdoing? How have you been punished?

7 Have you or others suffered as a consequence of your wrongdoing? In what ways?

8 Can you work out what the writer of the story believes about God?

9 What do you think that a member of the Jewish faith might learn from this story about looking after the world ?

10 What did you learn from this story?

RE Today
Services

Activity 2   Listen to the story of Genesis 1

Can you put the picture cards in the right order as you listen?

Strip 1 Sequence of Genesis 1	Strip 2 Sentence sequencing	Strip 3 Making sense/ interpretations	Strip 4 Questions to think about
Light	In the beginning God created the heavens and the earth.	Jewish people believe that The Eternal has always existed, since before the universe began.	Did the universe begin with light? What else might have come first?
Sea and sky	God separated the sky from the sea.	Jewish people give thanks to God for the sky above and the world below.	Would you like to be under the sea or high in the sky? Why?
Dry land: tree and leaf	God made every seed, flower and leaf, plant and tree.	In the Jewish faith, people praise God for the beauty of the earth	How is Harvest Thanksgiving connected to the creation story? What are your favourite plants?
Sun, moon and stars	A great light to rule the day and a silvery light to rule the night.	In olden days of Genesis, people worshipped the sun or the moon. But Jews worship the Invisible Almighty Creator.	Would God love the earth more than other planets, if the other planets have no life on them?
Birds and fish	The sky full of birds and the seas teeming full of fishes.	Birds and fish are different from human beings – they go where we cannot.	What are your favourite birds and fish in all creation?
Animals and humans	Every creeping thing on earth, beasts of the land and wild animals. Humanity, male and female, in God's own image.	Jewish people teach that the Almighty made human beings like the animals, but people were the best thing in all creation.	Is a human being more like an animal, or like God?
Rest	After all this work, REST.	Shabbat is a day of rest for Jewish people.	Do we need more rest in our own lives?

RE Today
Services

Activity 3 A Jewish story about the world's beginning: the second creation story in Genesis

When God first made the whole world, he planted a garden in the East. It was called the Garden of Eden, and it was very beautiful.

God took some dust and clay from the ground, and made a person. It was the very first man. God put him in the garden. The man worked for God, keeping the garden beautiful.

God's garden was amazing. All kinds of beautiful, fruity and flowering things grew there. Four lovely rivers flowed. In the middle of the garden was the awesome Tree of Knowledge.

The man gave names to all the animals in the garden. But there wasn't one which was his best friend, and God saw the man was lonely.

God sent a deep sleep on the man, and took one of his ribs. He made another person from the rib. She was the first woman. When the man woke up and saw her, he spoke the first poem.

God is generous. He gave the man and woman the garden. He told the man he could eat all the fruits except one. The only rule was: don't eat from the Tree of Knowledge. They wore no clothes, but felt happy like that.

In God's garden, the snake was the most crafty animal. He told Eve that God was a liar. 'You can eat from the Tree of Knowledge if you want.' Eve was tempted by the snake. Should she break God's rule?

Eve saw that the Tree of Knowledge had lovely fruit. She took some, and ate it. She offered some to Adam. He ate it too. Suddenly they both felt ashamed. They had broken God's one rule. They hid from God.

At the end of the day, God liked to walk in the garden. In the cool evening that night, he could not find Adam or Eve. He called out to them: 'Where are you?'

Adam and Eve made clothes from leaves. They didn't want to face God. They blamed each other, and the snake for breaking God's rule. God saw the truth: he gave them one rule, and they broke it.

God was sad, and angry. 'Now you will leave my beautiful garden,' he told them. 'You will have all kinds of troubles. You'll lose touch with me.' God said they would never come back.

Adam and Eve were full of sorrow. They left God's garden. Life was hard. Many sorrows came. But God kept an eye on them. He still loved the human race he had made. He still does.

Activity 6   Making sense of the story

Sort out these nine ideas about the story: which ones are best, do you think?

Work in a group of three:

- Use the 'Diamond 9' pattern to say what the story means.
- Which ideas are best?

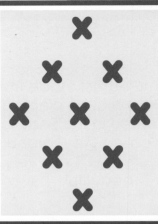

This story tells us the truth about our first parents – Adam and Eve.

This story is a bit like a parable – it's telling us that there is a good God who created everything. But we have the choice about whether we do good or evil.

This story shows that all people make bad choices sometimes.

Muslims, Jews and Christians love this story, so it's worth reading and talking about to find out why they like it so much.

Adam and Eve were real people.

The serpent is a symbol of the choice we all have to make between good and evil.

It's like an inner voice.

The story makes religious people think that they should help to look after God's creation.

We are meant to think that the serpent is a real one.

This old story isn't worth telling any more.

RE Today
Services

WHY CONTINUE BEING JEWISH? THE HOLOCAUST AND MEANINGFUL RE

For the teacher

Any study of the Holocaust should explore the richness and diversity of Jewish life and culture in Europe before the Second World War, as a reminder that Jewish people were and still are members of living, vibrant, thriving communities. Jewish people should always be represented and understood in the context of life and community rather than solely as victims.

Ideally a unit of work on the Holocaust should be cross-curricular. While History focuses on a study of the events of the past, it is the place of RE to grapple with the big questions about life and meaning, e.g. how is it possible to maintain a belief in God during times of suffering? RE is about meaning-making; this can also present a challenge as the Holocaust raises difficult questions about human behaviour.

The activities in this section provide ways for 9–11 year old pupils to explore Jewish beliefs and to express views about the role of faith during the Holocaust, linking this to their own ideas about the challenges of belonging to a religious tradition. Through the use of art, poetry and personal testimony, pupils will be encouraged to explore themes such as identity, belonging, stereotyping, persecution and hope.

Curriculum links

History: Impact of the Second World War

Literacy: Speaking and listening, biography and autobiography, poetry, diaries

PSHCE: Respecting the differences between people, recognising and challenging stereotypes, realising the nature and consequences of racism, teasing and bullying

Art and Design: Recording from experience and imagination, using a variety of materials to communicate ideas and feelings

What children can do as a result of this unit

The following pupil-friendly 'I can . . .' statements describe the learning that may be expected of pupils in the 9–11 age range.

Level Description of achievement: I can. . .

3
- describe two beliefs that are important in the Jewish tradition and say what a difference these beliefs made during the Holocaust
- *compare some of the beliefs that are important to me with those that influence Jewish people.*

4
- show that I understand some of the ways in which the events of the Holocaust had an impact on the faith of the Jewish people.
- *express my own questions and views about belonging to a group or religious tradition and suggest reasons why this may be difficult, referring to examples of Jewish people during the Holocaust.*

5
- suggest reasons why Jewish people may hold differing views about the importance of religious belief during the Holocaust
- *express my own views on questions about who we are and where we belong and explain the challenges of belonging to a religious tradition, taking account of Jewish responses during the Holocaust.*

Information file:

Who is a Jew?

According to Jewish religious law, a Jew is any person born of a Jewish mother or any person who chooses to become a Jew by converting to the Jewish religion.

According to the Nuremberg Laws, racial laws implemented by the German Parliament in Nuremberg on 15 September 1935, any person descended from at least three Jewish grandparents was considered a full-blooded Jew.

Many Jews living in Nazi-occupied Europe were not religious and considered themselves atheists, or assimilated or secular Jews; the anti-Jewish measures still affected them.

According to the 2001 UK Census, 267,373 people classified themselves as being Jewish.

See also

1 The Holocaust Centre, Laxton
Created for primary school children, 'The Journey' exhibition uses survivor testimony, film, photographs and artefacts to tell the journeys of Jewish children who lived through the Holocaust and survived, or who escaped from Nazi Germany before the war began.

See: www.holocaustcentre.net for information about how to visit.

2 *Journeys: Children of the Holocaust Tell Their Stories*, ed. Wendy Whitworth, ISBN 978-0-9555009-4-7. This collection of 30 brief testimonies of child survivors of the Holocaust is specially written for 10–11 year-old primary school children.

3 The Anne Frank House, Amsterdam: a website providing detailed information about the life of Anne Frank, including a timeline and the hiding place in 3D.

See: www.annefrank.org

4 'Let The World Read and Know' – The Oneg Shabbat Archives: a website providing information about Emanuel Ringelblum and photos, documents and diaries from the Archives.

See: www1.yadvashem.org/yv/en/exhibitions ringelbum/intro.asp

5 The Holocaust Educational Trust
The HET run a free-of-charge outreach programme, sending educators and Holocaust survivors into schools to teach about the Holocaust and explore its lessons in depth.

See: www.het.org.uk

Activity 1 What matters to me?

Ask pupils to:

- Use a diamond ranking to place the values below in order of importance in their life, from most important to least important.

- Get into groups of four and **explore** the following questions:

   ◦ Which value is at the top?
   ◦ Why is this most important in your life? Give reasons.
   ◦ What would you do if this value was challenged or taken away?
   ◦ How far would you go to uphold this value?
   ◦ Which value is at the bottom?
   ◦ Why is this least important in your life? Give reasons.
   ◦ What factors influenced your decision making?

- Have a **class discussion** about the placing of the values and **compare** ranking.

   ◦ Is there one value that appears overall as the most important?
   ◦ Which value is considered least important? Does it matter that our values may not be the same?

- **Reflect** on the diamond ranking activity and the discussion with other pupils to help you **create** your own charter of beliefs/values that are important in your life.

friends and family	education	food
religion	money	home
name	freedom	possessions

RE Today Services

Activity 2a   Jewish beliefs: persecution

Each of the six cards on page 28 provides a quotation from a Holocaust survivor describing the treatment of Jewish people living in Nazi-occupied Europe.

Pupils work in pairs or small groups.

Ask pupils to:

• **Read** each card carefully.

• **Create** a spider diagram to show the different ways in which Jewish people were being treated at this time.

• **Explore** the following questions:

  ◦ Which change do you think was the hardest to accept? Give reasons.

  ◦ Which change do you think was the easiest to accept? Give reasons.

  ◦ Why were Jewish people treated this way?

  ◦ How do you think the children felt to be Jewish at this time?

• **Think** of a time when you were treated differently or left out of a situation. How did it make you feel?

Activity 2b   Jewish beliefs: persecution

• **Discuss** ways in which people today are treated differently because of the religious tradition or group that they belong to.

• **Reflect** on the different ways that Jewish people were being persecuted in Nazi-occupied Europe. Display Psalm 23 from the Good News Bible and read it aloud. **Clarify** the meaning of any difficult words.

• **Suggest examples** of when the Jewish people may have experienced 'the deepest darkness' in their lives. In the original Hebrew text, it refers to 'the valley of the shadow of death'. Why is this phrase more pertinent when we are referring to the experience of the Jewish people?

• **Suggest ways** in which Psalm 23 could be a source of help and comfort for Jewish people such as Steven, Dorothy, John, Simon, Steve, Anne and Ellen during times of persecution.

• What difference do you think having a belief in God made at this time?

• Who or what gives you the strength to carry on in times of difficulty?

Activity 2c   Jewish beliefs: persecution

Pupils work individually or in pairs.

Ask pupils to:

• **Read** the quotes by Simon Winston, (page 30) and Anne Frank below. Both were in hiding during the Nazi occupation: Simon in Poland and Anne in the Netherlands.

• **Reflect** on the 'big' questions that Anne and Simon ask. What answers do they provide? Compare the differences and similarities in their thoughts about God.

• **Suggest reasons** why Anne Frank was able to retain her faith in God despite her suffering. Why do you think Simon began to express doubts about God?

• **Reflect** on your own beliefs about God. Do you relate more to Simon or Anne's views?

• **Explore** Simon's 'big' questions in more depth and attempt to provide answers to the following:

  ◦ Where was God?

  ◦ Why didn't God stop it?

• **Reflect** on what you have learned about the experience of Jewish people during the Holocaust. What 'big' questions would you like to ask?

Tuesday, 11 April 1944

'We must put our feelings aside; we must be brave and strong, bear discomfort without complaint, do whatever is in our power and trust in God. One day this terrible war will be over. The time will come when we'll be people again and not just Jews!

Who has inflicted this on us? Who has set us apart from all the rest? Who has put us through such suffering? It's God who has made us the way we are, but it's also God who will lift us up again.'

Anne Frank, from *The Diary of a Young Girl*. Used by permission.

When Hitler invaded Austria in 1938, I was already at High School, and I was planning to study there until I went to university. But things started to change. First of all the teacher made all the Jewish pupils, including me, sit at the back of the class, facing the wall. Then she told the other girls not to speak to us. Up to then, no one had paid any special attention to our religion. This sudden separation was hurtful and hard to understand. Then after summer 1938, Jewish children were no longer allowed to attend ordinary schools and my education stopped.

Dorothy Fleming

Jews also had to obey certain laws – we were not allowed to walk on the pavement or own a radio, and we had to wear a badge or armband to show we were Jewish. If we broke these laws, we weren't just fined or sent to prison; we we were shot dead. So we realised very quickly how bad our situation was.

Simon Winston

I remember while I was still at school that Jews were not allowed to go to the cinema or theatre, or take part in anything. I had a horrible experience at school. Our class was asked to give a radio performance and every girl was given a part to read, including me. I studied it, but then I was suddenly told, 'No! You can't take part in it, you're Jewish.' That really hurt at the time.

Ellen Rawson

After the Nazi invasion, I remember all the restrictions that changed my life and made me different from other children. First of all, I was no longer allowed to go to my nice modern primary school. I was sent to another school and the peculiar thing was that the people sitting next to me in class would be there one day, then disappear the next. They had been sent away by the Nazis 'to the east'. I wasn't allowed to play in the park at the end of the street, or go to the zoo or other places of entertainment. And I had to wear a yellow star to show that I was Jewish – even though my family wasn't religious at all.

Steven Frank

When I was five, my father was tickling me one day and I hit my head on the radiator. I had to go to the doctor's because I had cut my head. I remember the doctor said, 'That needs a stitch, but I don't stitch Jews. It will make my needle dirty.' So he put a plaster on it and today I've got a scar on my forehead.

John Fieldsend

Round about 1936 – just after the Olympic Games in Berlin – many of my friends suddenly started to ignore me. I challenged one of them to explain. He said, 'My father said I'm not allowed to play with Jews.' It was a bitter blow. My happy social life had been blown to bits. It was worse than being bullied because if someone bullies you, you can fight back. But if they ignore you completely, there's nothing you can do.

Steve Mendelsson

Quotations courtesy of the Holocaust Centre, Laxton

RE Today
Services

Activity 3   Jewish beliefs: art

Doris Weiserová was born on 17 May 1932 and deported to Terezin from Olomouc on 30 June 1942. She was sent to Auschwitz on 4 October 1944 where she died.

Pupils work in pairs or small groups with a copy of 'Passover Seder' (page 30).

Ask pupils to:

- **Analyse** the drawing and discuss what they can see.
  - What do you notice about the people?
  - What occasion are they celebrating?
  - How do you know?
- **Explain** how Doris drew this picture while she was imprisoned in the Terezin Ghetto. Doris could have chosen to draw anything.
  - Why do you think she chose to draw something that represented her religious beliefs?
  - How do you think her beliefs could have helped her at this time?
- **Consider** the significance of the festival of Passover for Jewish people.
  - Why is it of importance that Doris chose to focus her drawing on an event which celebrates freedom?
  - What words and images come to mind when you think of freedom?
- Children such as Doris often drew hope from their religious beliefs; festivals reminded them of happier times. **Discuss** what gives you hope and energy in your life.
- Provide the pupils with limited drawing materials and ask them to **create** a drawing/collage which depicts their own religious beliefs or what they draw hope and energy from in their lives.

Activity 4   Jewish beliefs: poetry

Franta (František) Bass was born in Brno on 4 September 1930. He was deported to Terezin on 2 December 1941, and died in Auschwitz on 28 October 1944. Franta wrote the poem, 'I am a Jew', while in the Terezin Ghetto.

Pupils work individually or in pairs.

Ask pupils to:

- **Read** the poem, 'I am a Jew', page 30. **Clarify** the meaning of any words that they are unsure of.
- **Explore** what the poem tells us about how Franta feels about being a Jew.
- **Reflect** on the line, 'I will always fight for my people'.
  - What beliefs do you hold that are worth fighting for?

Refer back to your charter of beliefs and values from Activity 1.

  - Which beliefs / values would you be willing to speak out for in public?
- **Write their own poem**, beginning with either the words, 'I am a . . .' describing how they feel about being a member of a religious tradition or 'I believe in . . .' to express something that they feel strongly about.

Page 30 can be downloaded by subscribers from the RE Today website.

Activity 5   Jewish beliefs: artefacts

The 'Oneg Shabbat' Archive (Hebrew: Sabbath pleasure) was a project established and run by Dr Emanuel Ringelblum in the Warsaw Ghetto. Ringelblum's aim was to produce a full picture of Jewish life under Nazi occupation, and all that was experienced, thought and suffered by the Jewish people. The archive, hidden in three milk cans, was to provide a detailed description of the fate of Jewish society. Show the picture on page 30.

Pupils work individually or in pairs.

Ask pupils to:

- **Discuss** what they think Jewish people at the time would have written about and contributed to the archive. If you were to document Jewish life today, what aspects of the Jewish tradition would you choose to preserve and why?
- **Think** about the difficulties of maintaining a religious life in these circumstances. Consider the following dilemmas that the Jewish people were faced with in the ghetto:

- Should one hold a Seder on Passover evening when there is no wine available and no matzot?
- Do you think the sick should be allowed to disregard the Sabbath?

How would a rabbi respond to these questions?

- **Describe** a time when it has been difficult for you to hold onto your beliefs. What did you do? How did it make you feel?
- **Imagine** the future of your own religious tradition or personal belief system was threatened. Using a shoebox, **compile** a collection of different items that you would save to ensure its continuation. **Compare** boxes with other pupils in the class. Which objects were considered the most/least important?
- **Reflect** on how the artwork, poem and artefacts help to express Jewish beliefs. What message do they convey about the importance of the continuation of the Jewish tradition?

Passover Seder, Doris Weiserová
Used by kind permission of the Jewish Museum in Prague

I am a Jew

I am a Jew and will be a Jew forever.
Even if I should die from hunger,
Never will I submit.
I will always fight for my people,
On my honour.
I will never be ashamed of them,
I give my word.
I am proud of my people,
How dignified they are.
Even though I am suppressed,
I will always come back to life.

Franta Bass
Used by kind permission of Pavel Uri Bass

I wanted to know where was God when this was happening? I wanted to know why didn't God stop it? Some of the most religious people, the most pious Jews, died first because they weren't useful to the German Nazi regime. Where was God to save them? At least, if we've done wrong, fine, but they had done nothing wrong, I kept asking God, I was talking to God but he wasn't talking back to me. So to some extent I'm still waiting for answers. But I've still got faith. I don't religiously go to the Synagogue, as I used to and even prayers are not that meaningful to me. But maybe one day all this can be explained to me one way or another.

Simon Winston

Metal utensils and milk containers in which part of the Oneg Shabbat archive was hidden, Warsaw, Poland.
Oneg Shabbat Archive

RE Today Services

REPRESENTING JUDAISM: TIPS FOR TEACHERS

In general

Judaism is the oldest of the monotheistic religions, which has spread worldwide. Judaism traces its origins back to the creation of humankind, but specifically Jewish history begins with Abraham and the Hebrew people. Jews believe that Abraham was called into a covenant, a binding agreement, with God to start a people whom God described as numbering as many as the stars in the sky.

Unlike some religions, Judaism does not choose to define itself in terms of beliefs, but rather on what Jewish people do to express their beliefs. Not all Jewish people are religious; by Jewish law, they are Jewish if they have formally converted to Judaism or if they were born to a Jewish mother. Some Jewish people choose not to adhere to specific religious beliefs and practices.

- Share with the pupils that Muslims and Christians also share many prophets and stories from the Torah. The three religions together are known as the 'people of the book'.

Key ideas in Judaism

Three areas of fundamental importance in Judaism are:

1 God

2 Torah

3 Land and the community

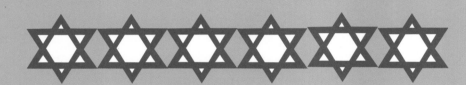

1 God

Jews believe in a creator God who made human beings in the image of himself. They believe that we cannot know what God looks like and so no pictorial representation of God will be found in synagogues or homes.

Many Jewish people believe the name of God is too sacred to pronounce. Jewish practice is to avoid writing the holy name of God, instead using 'G-d' in written form.

The words of the Shema are at the centre of Jewish belief. The opening of the Shema is:

'Hear O Israel, the Lord our G-d is one. Love the Lord your G-d with all your heart, with all your soul and with all your strength.'

2 Torah

The contents of the Torah are at the centre of Judaism. The written Torah and the oral Torah were given to Moses. The teaching in the Torah, which means instruction, contains 613 commandments.

Jews have other important teachings, which together make up the Tenakh or written Torah. These are:

- Torah – five books of Moses; these form the first five books of the Old Testament

- Nevi'im – the books of the Prophets

- Ketuvim – the holy writings.

The initials of each of these, T, N, K, make up the word Tenakh. Also important is the Talmud, which is known as the oral law.

3 Land and the community

Jewish identity is very important and at times this has been a challenge as Jews have faced oppression.

Judaism finds its roots in ancient Judea, now modern-day Israel. The nation state of Israel is considered to be the Jewish homeland and a holy site for Jews, wherever they live in the world. Jews believe God promised it to them through the promise to Abraham and his descendants. There are many sites of pilgrimage in Jerusalem, the most important of which is the Western Wall, which formed part of the second temple in Jerusalem.

The family and the wider Jewish community are central to living a practising Jewish life. Many Jewish festivals are based around the home as much as the synagogue, showing the importance of the family in Judaism.

RE Today
Services

Appropriate vocabulary

- God's name is treated with great respect in the Jewish tradition. The divine name, YHWH (Yahweh) is never pronounced. God is often referred to simply as Ha-Shem (the name).

- In prayer the Hebrew words 'Adonai' (the Lord) or 'Elohim' (the powerful) are used, these describe the characteristics of God rather than give a name.

- Some followers of the faith observe the practice further by not writing the full English word 'God' and substituting instead 'G-d' or 'Gd'. However, there is no Jewish law prohibiting the writing of the word 'God'.

- Pupils can be made aware of this feature in Jewish texts but do not need to replicate it in their own writing.

- Much of the Jewish vocabulary, which will be introduced to pupils, will be translated from the Hebrew. Written spellings vary.

- The word 'Jew' is not offensive but has been used at times in history as a derogatory term to show discrimination or prejudice against the Jewish race. To avoid this, where possible, use the term 'Jewish people'.

Useful websites and resources

Information sites for teachers written by Jewish people

See: www.jewfaq.org/index.htm

See: www.religionfacts.com/judaism/

This site has information for pupils and teachers with some ideas for teaching aspects of Judaism.

See: www.bbc.co.uk/schools/religion/judaism

The *Jewish Way of Life* CD-ROM is an excellent interactive resource introduced by two Jewish young people. The CD is free.

See: www.jwol.org.uk

Lisa Kassapian, RE Adviser

Diversity

- There are many different ways to practise Judaism, often referred to as 'movements'; examples of these would be Orthodox, Reform or Liberal. When teaching about the Jewish community, make it clear that Jews are, like other religions, a diverse community, practising in different ways.

- **Orthodox Judaism** has many different branches; these are unified by strict observance of the laws set out in the Torah.

- Jewish people from the **Liberal and Reform** tradition may believe that God's law as expressed in the Torah can be reintereped and brought up to date for today. The Reform movement were the first to ordain women rabbis. Both traditions have mixed seating in synagogues which marks the move towards greater gender equality.

- Among the more religiously observant Jews there is a strong ritualistic component, whereas other groups may tend to be more values focused. Ritual provides a mechanism to prompt values-driven behaviour; it is important to understand both.

- Teachers should ensure a balance of views when teaching Judaism. This multiplicity of ideas is fundamental to an understanding of the Jewish people.

- The synagogue provides a focus for prayer and learning, but the Jewish home perhaps gives an even greater perspective on Jewish life. Judaism is about a way of life.

- Prayer and synagogue attendance are not the only way in which Jews serve God: other ways are special meals, keeping kosher, saying blessings, certain dress codes and through interaction with others, influenced by Jewish ethical principles.

- Teaching about Judaism should not reduce this religion to lists of dates, festivals, practices and lifestyles, but also focus on providing active and engaging approaches, which facilitate learning from **Jewish values** and what constitutes **Jewish identity**.